MW01233299

DogeCoin

A Simple and Practical Guide to the Currency of the Future! Through well-structured steps you will learn: How, Why and Where to use this Currency that is revolutionizing the Cryptocurrency World.

JACOB LEWIS

by both the American Bar Association and the Committee of Publishers Association and is legally binding throughout the United States.

Furthermore, the transmission, duplication, or reproduction of any of the following work including specific information will be considered an illegal act irrespective of if it is done electronically or in print. This extends to creating a secondary or tertiary copy of the work or a recorded copy and is only allowed with the express written consent from the Publisher. All additional right reserved.

The information in the following pages is broadly considered a truthful and accurate account of facts and as such, any inattention, use, or misuse of the information in question by the reader will render any resulting actions solely under their purview. There are no scenarios in which the publisher or the original author of this work can be in any fashion deemed liable for any hardship or damages that may befall them after undertaking information described herein.

Additionally, the information in the following pages is intended only for informational purposes and should thus be thought of as universal. As befitting its nature, it is presented without assurance regarding its prolonged validity or interim quality. Trademarks that are mentioned are done without written consent and can in no way be considered an endorsement from the trademark holder.

Table of Content

INTRODUCTION

In this guide, we will shed light on all the aspects of Dogecoin that are worth evaluating before making any investments. Beyond the speculative aspect, however, we will also look at the technology and the ultimate purpose of this project. The goal is to satisfy potential investors.

Not only Bitcoin and Ethereum. To take off, in recent months, even the unpredictable Dogecoin, the cryptocurrency created in 2013 in the image and likeness of a popular meme. What it is, how it works, how to buy: here's everything you need to know.

Dogecoin continues to hold sway among cryptocurrency enthusiasts and investors looking for profits. And to say so, without risk of denial, are the numbers themselves. A year ago the currency was traded at 0.0019 dollars, at a sidereal distance from Bitcoin and the first Altcoins by market cap, but with the favorable wind of the last year straight in the sails the crypto ended up making a rise (monstrous) of 13,573%, even breaking the quota of 0.4 dollars before retracing. A path that has no equal among the albeit performing BTC & Co.

But what is it, exactly, this Dogecoin? How does it work? And how can you buy it? Below is a complete guide.

CHAPTER 1

DOGECOIN: WHAT IS IT AND HOW IT WORKS

Dogecoin, as mentioned, is a cryptocurrency created in 2013, in Oregon. It was still the first republic of social, and the Internet community had long been circulating a meme depicting a Shiba Inu, Japanese dog breed. From there, a certain Billy Markus was inspired to merge the embryonic interest in virtual currencies, which was already mounting, with the proverbial irreverence of the web, giving birth to a sort of crypto-meme, the Dogecoin.

In short, a joke, which however has been transformed, year after year, into something real, serious, tangible, and now worth almost 50 billion dollars. Incredible, given the premises, but there you go.

From a purely technical point of view, however, Dogecoin is a pure cryptocurrency, meaning it is used exclusively to make payments. In this sense, it is similar to Bitcoin, but profoundly different, in terms of logic and nature, from currencies like Ethereum and Ripple, which put transactions in the background. Basically, then, Dogecoin allows you to buy goods or services with a decentralized, secure payment method with low fees.

There is no shortage of thorns, however. And the main one, at a time of renewed interest in eco-sustainability issues, is related to the way tokens are mined. Dogecoin uses in fact, like Bitcoin, a proof-of-work verification model, which basically puts miners in competition with each other, with enormous computing power used, huge consumption of electricity and enormous damage to the environment.

CHAPTER 2

HOW TO BUY DOGECOIN

Let's start by saying that this is a "pure" cryptocurrency, meaning it is used exclusively to make payments. In this it is similar to Bitcoin, but different from other projects such as Ethereum or Ripple where the transaction aspect is secondary.

Now, for those who are interested in buying Dogecoin and ride the success of the last year, there is good news: the operation is simple and takes a few minutes. But how to do it? In addition to mining them directly, the direct way to get the crypto passes through the exchanges, the platforms that quote the main virtual currencies.

It will be enough, therefore, to create an account on one of the exchanges that offer Dogecoin - such as, for example, Kraken, Binance or Bittrex - and insert a payment

method (on the platforms

cryptocurrencies are exchanged against

fiat currencies, such as euros or dollars).

There are two alternatives: credit card, to

buy Dogecoin quickly and act instantly on

the market, or bank transfer, mainly to

save on commissions.

CHAPTER 3

IS DOGECOIN A SCAM?

Many times we hear Dogecoin associated

with the idea of jokes and irony, which

might lead some to think that it is a hoax

or a scam. The fact that this brand has

decided to address the market with

sympathy, however, is only meant to

emphasize the simple nature of this token

and the fact that it is affordable for

anyone.

Beyond the Doge mascot, however, this is a very serious reality. This crypto steadily occupies a place among the 25 most capitalized decentralized coins ever.

Dogecoin's community is also quite large. For those who don't know, the websites where cryptocurrency developers and experts aggregate the most are Reddit, GitHub and BitcoinTalk Forum.

On all three of these channels, Dogecoin enjoys great fame and reputation. You only need to use some exchanges to convert dollars into Dogecoin and vice versa to verify that everything is working smoothly, which I wanted to try before writing this guide.

WHY DOGECOIN ?

By now, the existing cryptocurrencies are countless, in the order of magnitude of thousands. In such a large market, it is not always easy to identify the projects that can succeed and that, compared to the most capitalized, have structural advantages that can help them emerge.

Dogecoin is built on a technological infrastructure that basically resembles that of Bitcoin, but with some important differences that mark a huge step forward on a technological level.

First of all, thanks to the transaction verification protocol, it only takes one minute for a transaction to be verified and added to the blockchain. It's certainly not the shortest time possible, but it's certainly much better than what Bitcoin and Litecoin allow us to do. Also, there is no maximum number of minable Dogecoins: again unlike BTC and LTC, in this case the supply is unlimited.

Besides all this, the most important thing

to point out is that Dogecoin is one of the most traded cryptocurrencies ever. We are not talking about speculative movements, which according to most analysts' estimates account for more than 90% of transactions; in this case we are referring to all those people who actually use.

Dogecoin to send and receive money in exchange for goods or services. In the long run, the popularity of a cryptocurrency within the real economy will be what really makes the difference. For now, it is still rare to find companies and stores that allow us to pay with virtual currencies, but among those that do allow it, there are many that accept Dogecoins.

THE LIMITS OF DOGECOIN

Although in many ways this crypto has a lot of potential, there are some obvious limitations of this project that should be overcome. First among them is the way tokens are mined: there is an analogy here with Bitcoin, as both cryptocurrencies use the proof-of-work verification model.

If you don't know what that means, we'll give you a brief description here; the full explanation, along with all the comparisons to other mining systems, can be found in the guide to cryptocurrency consensus protocols.

In the proof-of-work verification model,miners must lend their computing power to the network by competing with each other. They have to make sure that they cryptograph first, in the correct way, the new blocks to be added to the blockchain.

A lot of computing power is required for each block, which translates into significant costs for electricity and equipment dedicated to mining;

electricity, in turn, has a strong environmental impact. It's no coincidence that many times the Dogecoin community has proposed, on Reddit and other channels, to move to a proof-of-stake verification model like Ethereum's.

Unfortunately, up to this point, things have not changed, and Dogecoin's last substantial technology upgrade now dates back to 2015. Cryptocurrencies with PoW technology appear anachronistic and outdated, so this will be a big challenge to

overcome.

IS IT WORTH INVESTING IN DOGECOIN?

This is a very difficult question, because on

the one hand there are all the great

advantages of this project and on the

other there is one fundamental limitation.

The problem is that, since there is now a

wide choice of tokens on the market, a

single macroscopic flaw can make investors pass the desire to believe in a project.

Surely the ease of use of this cryptocurrency, coupled with its wide popularity, could contribute to an increase in its value and its diffusion in the real economy.

The counterbalance to this discourse is a transaction verification model that is no longer in step with the times.

Projects like Tron and Ethereum are becoming increasingly popular precisely because of the PoS protocol, which allows them to verify transactions and add them to the blockchain in seconds. We can wish the best for the future of this project, but it is very likely that its structural limitations will prevent it from entering the top 10 most capitalized cryptocurrencies.

WHAT IS A
FINANCIAL BUBBLE?

Let's remember that a financial bubble is a

typical phenomenon of the markets, which

concerns the rise in price of an asset

supported mainly by speculative interests

within it. This leads to further price

increases, and therefore, to a further

growth of interest around it.

A vicious circle that sooner or later is

destined to collapse because it is not

supported by a real intrinsic value of the asset.

Historically, clamorous examples of financial bubbles are those of tulip seeds in Holland (at the beginning of 1600, first case in history) or the dot-com case, in 2000, related to technology stocks.

DOGECOIN BUBBLE ABOUT TO BURST?

Now, however, many are wondering if Dogecoin is a financial bubble. Kind of the same question that was asked when certain rises it was Bitcoin that first registered in 2017.

Right now, there are very few use cases for the token. Although more merchants are starting to accept dogecoin as a payment method, it's nowhere near the level of adoption needed to be used as any

kind of effective currency substitute.

"It's all a big marketing ploy these days,"

said Mike Bucella, general partner at

BlockTower Capital.

Unlike rival cryptocurrencies like Ethereum

- which allows programmers to create

applications on their platform to do things

like lend and borrow money - there's not

much anyone can do with dogecoin.

Dogecoin isn't even a true store of wealth, as that typically requires some degree of long-term trust in the coin and the blockchain on which it's built.

"If you look at the dogecoin protocol itself, I don't even know if there's anyone in the last few years that has added new features or code," Birla said. "Dogecoin doesn't really have a development team behind it."

Given these limitations, the run-up in dogecoin seems to be purely speculative. Dogecoin has value because other people believe it has value. And because they believe someone else is willing to buy it from them at a higher price.

Former Federal Reserve Chairman Alan Greenspan is very skeptical: "We see the rise in the price of dogecoin as a factor of low liquidity and extreme growth in the network," explained Alan Greenspan.

"Once the network reaches critical mass, I don't think that kind of growth is sustainable."

However, Bucella also believes that "The real value is in today's meme-driven culture, and doge represents the network value of memetics, which could prove to be huge."

CHAPTER 4

ELON MUSK AND THE DOGECOIN

Returning to the market movements of

Dogecoin, there is no doubt that much of

the rise of the crypto is due to the social

incontinence of Elon Musk, number one of Tesla and SpaceX, who for months has been trying to push his followers, with a barrage of tweets, to bet on the asset.

In fact, behind almost all the stretches of the currency, from a year ago, there has been a tweet of the tycoon, and even today it is not clear if the continuous endorsements of the brilliant - but controversial - "technoking" respond to a concrete interest in Dogecoin or are just a way (veiled) to take the market by the nose.

It is a fact, in any case, that Elon Musk is inextricably linking his name to that of the currency, and that, on the occasion of several interviews, he has spoken of Dogecoin as his favorite crypto. And, between the serious and the facetious, the quotation continues to swell.

DOGECOIN, THE REASONS FOR THE LATEST BOOM

Dogecoin, the reasons for the latest boom.

And the Musk factor, on closer inspection,

is also behind the latest boom of Dogecoin.

In ten days the crypto has gained 457%,

going from 0.061 to 0.34 dollars. An

exploit that, in addition to the tweets of

the tycoon ("Doge Barking at the Moon"

was Musk's last post on Twitter), can

undoubtedly be ascribed also to the

Coinbase IPO, the exchange that last week

debuted on Nasdaq and rewarded, in

cascade, almost all crypto.

MUSK STRIKES AGAIN AND SENDS THIS STOCK INTO A TAILSPIN

Elon Musk intervenes - again - on Twitter

and pushes in orbit a stock: which one?

Continues the financial influence and

meddling in the markets by the patron of

Tesla, hits of simple tweets.

Elon Musk tries again, perhaps unwittingly, and sends a stock into orbit on the South Korean Stock Exchange.

The CEO of Tesla continues to pose as a true influencer of investors and this time, always with the weapon of a tweet, he made a Korean company take off.

What happened and what did Musk say to affect the markets?

MUSK SENDS A TWEET AND PUSHES THIS STOCK UP +10%

The mechanism is already known: Elon Musk proposes his comment on Twitter and the financial markets respond.

Cryptocurrencies such as bitcoin and dogecoin have previously seen sharp changes in their prices following the tech billionaire's comments.

His tweets have also previously been linked to moves in the stock market in so-called meme stocks like GameStop.

This time the shares of Samsung Publishing, a major shareholder of the producer of the children's song "Baby Shark", are benefiting from the rise.

After a tweet about the viral ditty, the stock shot up. Samsung Publishing's shares in South Korea rose more than

10% at one point during regular trading on Wednesday, before equalizing some gains to close 6.29% higher.

The company has no affiliation with South Korean conglomerate Samsung Group, though it shares the Samsung name.

Wednesday's gains came on the heels of a tweet from Musk on Tuesday morning, Asian time, that read, "Baby Shark crushes everything! More views than humans."

Samsung Publishing's stock is up more than 76 percent in 2018 after the song "Baby Shark" smashed the charts in the U.K. and went viral.

CHAPTER 5

HERE'S WHY DOGECOIN IS A CRYPTOCURRENCY TO BUY CAREFULLY

Dogecoin as the other cryptocurrencies had a sudden growth due to the positive statements of Elon Musk on these coins, however, in a short time has also recorded a relevant collapse: let's see what happened and what are the characteristics of this currency.

Dogecoin went in a very short time from a sudden growth of more than 65% in a few days, until February 7, to a collapse that in the space of seven hours touched 23% (on February 15). An emblematic case of how much the extreme volatility of cryptocurrencies on the market makes them still accessible to few, although their history - see Bitcoin - is convincing more and more institutions and big players (Tesla) to consider them now reliable at least in the long term.

DOGECOIN AND BITCOIN, THE INFLUENCE OF ELON MUSK

Just in the last period many cryptocurrencies have reached very high peaks but also important downsizing all because of one person, Elon Musk of Tesla, precisely. As you know, Musk a few days ago had made it known that Tesla, the

Californian company of electric cars, had invested 1.5 billion in bitcoin and that in the near future it intends to accept them as a means of payment for its products.

The trend of the cryptocurrency, already particularly volatile, jumped 10% to a record of over $44,000. In addition to this, a series of other tweets of the founder of Tesla have caused a real surge of other cryptocurrencies such as Dogecoin, shot up by 65% in 24 hours, thanks also to contributions of support from artists such as Snoop Dog and Gene Simmons of Kiss. Specifically, just a week before, Musk had written on Twitter that bitcoin, and in full the concept of cryptocurrency, was about to be widely accepted among investors. This could represent a genuine turning point between those who never believed much in digital currencies and those who instead believed in them from the very first moment. A statement like this, in fact, for better or worse turns the spotlight on the topic in an unequivocal way.

Musk then also tweeted that he bought

Dogecoin for his son.

Elon Musk ✅
@elonmusk

Bought some Dogecoin for lil X, so he can be a
toddler hodler

4:08 PM · Feb 10, 2021

♡ 547.5K   💬 28.7K   🔗 Copy link to Tweet

WHY THE DROP IN DOGECOIN

Currently, however, the value of the cryptocurrency Dogecoin has plummeted by 23%. How is such a sudden drop possible? The reason is soon identified and it pertains to the topic of coin distribution. Specifically, Dogecoin has one of the most unequal coin distributions in the cryptocurrency world. 28.7% is held by one person, while the next 12 users own almost 50% of the supply.

This situation, prompted Elon Musk to tweet the following, "If the top Dogecoin holders sell most of their coins, you will have my full support. In my opinion, overconcentration is the only real problem." In just over 7 hours, the price of the cryptocurrency has plummeted 23%, from $0.063 to $0.048.

Elon Musk ✔
@elonmusk

If major Dogecoin holders sell most of their coins, it will get my full support. Too much concentration is the only real issue imo.

12:25 AM · Feb 15, 2021   ⓘ

♡ 329.9K   💬 28.5K   🔗 Copy link to Tweet

PRICE AND VALUE OF DOGECOIN IN DOLLARS

For example, as seen in the chart,

Dogecoin's peak was close to $0.1 and

then fell to $0.05 on February 16.

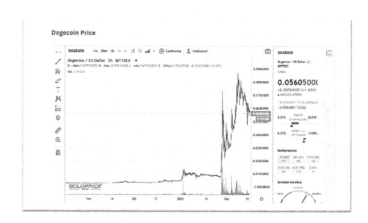

DOGECOIN, FUNDRAISING

In particular, the most relevant fundraising campaigns referred to are three.

- The Doge4Water campaign, which was based on the desire to build a water collection basin in Kenya, near the Tana River. In this nation, so deeply affected by poverty, a realization of this kind has proved invaluable.

- The campaign raised funds for the Family House, which provides support for families of children with cancer or other similar illnesses. This was a campaign that raised a lot of public awareness and made the cryptocurrency very popular.

- The fundraising campaign to enable the Jamaican bobsled team to participate in the Winter Olympics.

All these charitable initiatives have certainly contributed, all other things being equal with its competitors, to increase the awareness and relevance of Dogecoin.

OTHER WEAKNESSES OF DOGECOIN

There have been, however, some hot issues about this cryptocurrency that have nothing to do with the fundraising campaigns that made it famous. In addition to the already in-depth volatility, one issue is related to a structural weakness that in the outlook is likely to strongly penalize this cryptocurrency at the expense of its competitors.

Its founder, Jackson Palmer, has admitted that for this virtual currency, born for fun and become one of the most important on the market, there are no innovations of a technical nature. This will obviously make it difficult for Dogecoin to keep up with the competition. Although the latter has, to date, a capitalization that exceeds six billion dollars, it is still a relevant issue to be taken into account if you decide to invest in this digital currency.

CHAPTER 6

BITCOIN, LITECOIN AND DOGECOIN HERE ARE THE DIFFERENCES BETWEEN THE 3 CRYPTOCURRENCIES

In these days we talk more and more about cryptocurrencies, object of attention from the most important international media. Cryptocurrencies have in fact gone from being an obscure part of finance to finding themselves at the center of the scene and the debate in the last year. In the space of 12 months, the value of bitcoin has exploded from $8,166 on March 8, 2020 to historic highs of over $58,000 in February 2021, which may soon be exceeded again.

The rapid rise of cryptocurrencies has been accompanied by growing institutional interest, including from big names like Goldman Sachs, BNY Mellon, JP

Morgan and Paypal. There are hundreds of

cryptocurrencies around the world, but 20

of them make up about 99% of the market

volume. These include Litecoin and

Dogecoin.

BITCOIN, THE MOTHER OF ALL CRYPTOCURRENCIES

Bitcoin was the first cryptocurrency, and its founding principles were enunciated by Satoshi Nakamoto in a 2008 paper titled "Bitcoin: A Peer-to-Peer Electronic Cash System." Nakamoto described the project as "an electronic payment system based on cryptographic proof instead of trust."

Cryptographic evidence comes in the form

of transactions that are verified and recorded, as noted above, in the network called the blockchain. A blockchain is a kind of open electronic ledger that records transactions in code. Transactions are recorded in "blocks" that are then linked together in a "chain" of previous cryptocurrency transactions.

THE LITECOIN, "THE DIGITAL SILVER"

Litecoin was created by Charlie Lee in October 2011. Since that date, the asset has consistently been among the top 10 largest cryptocurrencies by market capitalization. Litecoin was one of the very first altcoins on the market. While many altcoins from 2011-2013 are now gone, Litecoin has remained on the market thanks to some small but still useful and well-considered changes from Bitcoin.

Litecoin is close to Bitcoin in many features, but has some key differences.

Among them:

- A "working proof" that uses the scrypt hash function instead of SHA-256.

- Four times faster block creation with an average interval of 2.5 minutes instead of 10 minutes.

- A four-fold increase in the total number of units, from 21 million to 84 million.

- A mining difficulty that changes every two and a half days instead of every two weeks.

DOGECOIN, A JOKE COME TRUE

The Dogecoin (DOGE) is an open source, peer-to-peer cryptocurrency. It is considered an altcoin and an almost sarcastic meme coin. Launched in December 2013, Dogecoin has an image of a Shiba Inu dog as its logo. Although it was created ostensibly as a joke, Dogecoin's blockchain still has interesting features. Its core technology is derived from Litecoin. Two significant features of

Dogecoin are its low price and unlimited supply.

Dogecoin is also known for being referred to as his "favorite cryptocurrency" by Tesla patron Elon Musk on Twitter. The hype fueled by the numerous memes about Dogecoin, at one point pushed it into the top ten most valuable cryptocurrencies, eventually prompting official recognition, even by major exchange sites, of what started out as a simple joke.

CONCLUSIONS

The growing attention towards cryptocurrencies, also by banks and international bodies that initially showed great diffidence towards them, has favored a growth in their value that at the moment does not seem to stop. Analysts are wondering at the moment, with conflicting answers, what could be the maximum peak of this rise, starting with Bitcoin, before a downsizing. What is certain is that this is a phenomenon with which all financial institutions, even those traditionally more hostile, must now deal.

CPSIA information can be obtained
at www.ICGtesting.com
Printed in the USA
BVHW091922240621
610211BV00016B/1906